Start of the Coming Civil War

MARK WROBEL

Start of the Coming Civil War

By Mark Wrobel

Cover Created & Designed by Jazzy Kitty Publications

Logo Designs by Andre M. Saunders/Jess Zimmerman

Editor: Anelda L. Attaway

© 2020 Mark Wrobel

ISBN 978-1-7357874-9-7

Library of Congress Control Number: 2020925512

All rights reserved. This book is protected by the copyright laws of the United States of America. This book may not be copied or reprinted for commercial gain or profit. The use of short quotations or occasional page copying for personal or group study is permitted and encouraged. Permission will be granted upon request. This book is for Worldwide Distribution and printed in the United States of America, published by Jazzy Kitty Publications utilizing Microsoft Publishing Software.

ACKNOWLEDMENT & DEDICATION

First and foremost, I acknowledge God and thank Him for sustaining me through life with my disability.

I dedicate this book to my publisher Mrs. Anelda Attaway known to many as Jazzy Kitty, as a thank you for publishing my books. Mrs. Anelda was professional and supportive throughout the entire process. She made my dream of becoming a published author come true. I don't know how I would have done this with her and the Jazzy Kitty Publications staff.

TABLE OF CONTENTS

INTRODUCTION..i
CHAPTER 1 – The Seeds of the New American War............................01
CHAPTER 2 – The Black Community in America Today......................04
CHAPTER 3 – The Education System in America Today.....................09
CHAPTER 4 – The Communist are Coming..15
CHAPTER 5 – No Gold in Fort Knox..19
CHAPTER 6 – The Chipping of Humanity...22
CHAPTER 7 – Second Amendment Under Threat...............................25
CHAPTER 8 – Who Stands Behind our President?..............................28
CHAPTER 9 – Control of the Population by the Rich and Powerful.....31
CHAPTER 10 – Mind Control Experiments on the American People...35
CHAPTER 11– The First Earth Battalion..38
CHAPTER 12 – 9/11 was an Inside Job...40
CHAPTER 13 – The Fall of the Republic..43
ABOUT THE AUTHOR..51
REFERENCES..53

INTRODUCTION

I am writing this book with a heavy burden because of the death of Democracy in America. There is no way to avoid the upcoming Civil War. Therefore, the purpose of this book is to prepare the American citizens for what's coming in this country.

This book will show and explain the causes of this upcoming Civil War in America. You must know this to survive what is coming and what will happen in the United States. This book will prepare you mentally and physically to have some control over yourself and your family during this unavoidable turmoil.

The people who died in 9/11 are demanding the truth and seeking justice. Anyone who has stolen anything from the American people should give it back while they are alive because they will have to give it back after death.

CHAPTER 1

The Seeds of the New American Civil War

In this chapter, we will examine the issues that might lead to the new American Civil War; there are many of them. One of them is that the people will no longer elect the president in elections. Most of the time, the president, with maybe one exception Donald J. Trump has been selected by special interests such as the Builder Burg Group and many others. That is why it is essential to inform people to keep an eye on our elected representatives.

In my opinion, Donald Trump tried to do an excellent job as president when he said to build that wall. I think that the major puppet masters behind the throne have taken control of our government under President Trump. Here is where President Trump fell into the trap that was set up by the puppet masters. We all remember all of those Caravans that were walking towards the American border from South America. Well, unfortunately, President Donald Trump was unable to stop all those hordes. Those Caravans have disappeared from our news and television screens. The situation is not getting better because Globalists and organizations are helping those illegal immigrants. As you know, Joe Biden is the president-elect, and that is what the American people wanted to do is elect a Democrat.

The next questions should be, when did the seeds of the next American Civil War start to be planted and by whom? Here I'm going to give you a list of people who began planting the seeds of the next Civil War in America.

The first person responsible for the next American Civil War is

Timothy Leary. He was a big advocate of drugs (hard drugs) to make the population dumbed down and be a compliant sheep to Global Governance. (Wikipedia, n.d.)

The second person responsible for our next Civil War would be **William Kunstler**. He was a lawyer for the Communist Party USA in the late 1950s and 60s. (Wikipedia, n.d.)

The third organization responsible for the fall and planning the next American Civil War seeds is the **Communist Party USA** (htt1). As you can see by now, most of those organizations started to tear America down in the late 50s and early 60s.

Now we will move into the discussion about peace marches back in the 1960s. After careful analysis of peace marches or so-called peace marches back in the 1960s, they were never about ending the Vietnam War. They were all about taking the system down and destroying America as a sovereign nation. Looking at those who took part in those marches back in the 1960s had good intentions. Nevertheless, sometimes the road paved by good intentions has the opposite effects.

Remember this, if you think the Left-wingers' attacks have ended in the late 70s on our nations' governing system, you are greatly mistaken. That's because those who were part of the Left-wing/Communist Movement had descendants. Those children of the old hippies have picked up the mental of the so-called American Revolution. I will tell you that any revolution will not lead to anything good. Because in a Communist/Socialist Society, those at the top of the system before the revolution will also be there after the revolution and beyond. But, that person on the bottom before the revolution can end up in the worst shape afterward.

The other person responsible for the turmoil that we are experiencing in America today is **George Soros**. (Wikipedia, n.d.)

Unfortunately, there is more bad news on the horizon until the president restores order and tranquility in this country. America, as a nation, will slip into anarchy and then cease to exist. You might have a question right about now, what can the president do to restore peace and prosperity to the United States? Until the United States President takes some drastic measures to restore civility in this nation, nothing will change. People that are behind the riots must be arrested, brought to trial, and put in jail. As of this writing, all those who are rioting in the streets are not the actual people behind the curtain. That is because for the peace and tranquility to be restored on our streets, of course, those mobs who are looting stores, burning down our buildings and churches must be put down and severely punished. The people who burnt down the churches and looting the stores are only peons or pawns in the bigger picture. The bigger problem is if the people in our government do not restore order, the American citizens will take on the restoration to our streets upon themselves and believe me, you and I do not want to see that happen. That is because the New World Order puppet masters are just waiting for something like that to happen. After all, they can implement their plan which is not good. There used to be a saying, *"If the leaders will not lead, then we, the people, must lead our leaders."* Therefore, if the people who are supposed to lead cannot do their job, then it is up to us to restore order to our streets.

CHAPTER 2

The Black Community in America Today

I watched those riots in the streets and I find something very peculiar about them. Those rioters are burning down and looting the stores in their neighborhoods. More perplexing is that those rioters and looters are looting and burning the property in their Black communities.

Now you might be asking the question at this time. Why are you picking on the Black community? There is one single reason for that and it's because where is the so-called Black leadership such as the Rev. Jackson, Rev. Sharpton, and the rest of those so-called Black leaders? The Black community will say that no one wants to invest in Black neighborhoods. This is going to happen right after the riots. Think about this for a minute, if you were an investor and you had 100 million dollars to invest in a Black neighborhood after the riots, knowing that the same thing might happen in a couple of years; would you invest the money for a business in a community like that?

You see, as we look at and examine the Black leadership in America today like Reverend Jessie Jackson and Al Sharpton, which I think they are not Black leaders. They are nothing more than a bunch of race hustlers who make money and put Black against White so they can make more money on the turmoil between the races.

Remember this; those people are also puppets used to move us into the global New World Order. I love how the race hustlers always love to say that the Black community has no good role models to follow. Believe me; I'm going to show you how the race hustlers are wrong in this case.

Here is a list of role models that might have some good influence on the Black community.

Mary Jackson, who is she? She was the first Black woman to be a NASA engineer/mathematician who helped in figuring out that trajectory of the space rocket going to the moon. The reason I like her is that she worked hard for everything that she earned. She did not bellyache about give me this or that because somebody owes me something. I have to admit that she had to work extra hard to achieve what she wanted. No matter how hard the dream was for her to succeed, she showed everyone that no matter how challenging the situation is in your life, you have to overcome it, and you can too achieve your dreams. (Wikipedia, n.d.)

The next role model is **Frederick Douglass**. He was a Civil Rights Leader in the late 1800s. Even Frederick has predicted our situation and today's America and Black communities. However, in today's Black society, Frederick Douglass does not get the respect that he deserves. (Wikipedia, Wikipedia, n.d.) Frederick Douglass has warned the Black community about the race hustlers of today.

The third and final role models that the Black community should try to emulate are the **Tuskegee Airmen**. The Tuskegee Airmen are just like everyone above on these particular lists; they had to overcome many different things. The Tuskegee Airmen have achieved their dreams to fly airplanes. Most of those men had college degrees and they earned those degrees by sure determination and willpower. They did not say that this is impossible; they overcame any obstacles that faced them to achieve their goals. (htt2)

Today, I notice the Black community is the phenomenon that young Black man would follow and emulate which is the lowest common denominator. I know what your next question is going to be; what are you talking about? What is the lowest common denominator?

You see, today's Black community rather follow gangster rappers who wear their caps backward and wear their pants without belts down to their knees. I know where this kind of gangster culture came from. It came from the prison system. My question to the Black community is, why are some people in the Black community emulating and imitating the world's most destructive culture?

Even in some of the rap music today, every other word is *MY MOTHER IS A HO*. My question is, have the Black parents abdicated the role of raising their kids or have they turned to state to raise their kids? I know that some of the so-called, Black leadership will take offense to what I have said in this chapter. Most importantly, I know that they'll come up with 100 excuses why is this happening. I know or think I know one of the excuses which is there are no fathers in their home. This is no excuse for what is happening in the Black community today because it is still the parent's responsibility to have their kids home by 10 pm and not rioting, burning down buildings, and other things. In this case, the fathers and mothers in the Black community should take responsibility for their children's behavior in the streets today. I know that the so-called Black leadership will attack me and discredit me.

The next excuse they are going to use is White privilege. Well, let me tell you about my White privilege. First, I am an immigrants son; my father worked as a construction worker so that we could have a better life. I spent most Saturday's in the winter with my father on a construction site; nobody gave me anything for free. Being an immigrants son, I did not have an easy time when I was young. I am not here to bellyache about this or that. I've hard work and had determination to achieved everything in the military or my university education. And believe me, there were undoubted obstacles in my life that stood in my way of achieving my goals.

Most of the people who stood in my way of achieving my dreams were my grade and high school teachers—especially the guidance counselors who were no help. My guidance counselors and other school officials have made me attend Special Education Classes because I was learning slowly. The fact is, we are all different; some are skinny, some are fat, some are Black, and some are White. Therefore, we have different speeds that we learn things, which is a very good thing because this is the way it's supposed to be. We cannot be all the same, because if that is the case, think about how boring the world would be.

Nowadays, I have achieved most of my educational dreams because many people, teachers, and the school told me that I will not earn a college degree. But boy, I have proven them all wrong! Therefore, there is no such thing as a White privilege; in my opinion, there's only laziness and wanting something for nothing. That is why I like America because lots of people have taught me that there is no such thing as a *"FREE LUNCH."* In America, nothing is given to you outright; you must put in the hard work to achieve something great.

From time to time, I am angry at the American education system, as well. That is because the education system did not support me in achieving my dream of completing my college degree nor becoming a great writer. Nevertheless, I did not let that stop me from achieving my goals. The more people told me that I could not do something, the more I wanted to prove them wrong. That has driven me to succeed and I did not make excuses or complained that someone owes me something.

CHAPTER 3

The Education System in America Today

Politicians in America have talked about reforming and bringing our education system into the 21st Century. But this has not been successful for many years. We all know that the education system in the United States today does not meet the academic standards nor help students to be successful in their lives after high school or college.

President Donald Trump's daughter, Ivanka Trump, says, "College is not the only way to achieve success," and to some degree she is correct. Due to future employers' demands *"that I have mentioned in my previous book,"* eventually, those who work in the trades field will be expected to have some type of college degree. I am not putting down all of our tradesmen; the future college degree demands will eventually be a must. For college students to be successful, the college and university system must be reformed. You might be asking yourself right now. How can we achieve this?

There is a variety of ways of doing this in which I list below:

1. We have to reform our college and university system to cut back on the number of peripheral subjects.

Here is how this would work; for example, if you are majoring in IT and Computer Science, we should emphasize learning about this subject of computers in today's colleges. Of course, yes, you are going to learn about Computer Science. But, before you get into those particular subjects, you must take some of those peripheral classes such as English, three mathematical classes, literature classes, and some other thing that has the "word" studies after it.

President Donald Trump said we he was in office that we need more computer engineers to compete with China. Also, we will need more computer hackers. In this case, I did support him in this endeavor. Yet, this may not work too well. Suppose you are spending more time on your peripheral classes such as English literature. In that case, you are spending less time on your major subjects such as Computer Science subjects. While President Donald Trump was in office he wanted to win the war against China. Therefore, he should've pressured the Science departments, such as Robotics and the Computer departments. So that college students when they get out into the real world can compete in the job market and the global economy that we will have to face.

We also must put the brakes on the sports programs in our colleges and universities because we will not fight against China with firearms. We will have to win this war with our brainpower. Therefore, we should not emphasize sports. Also, you hear of the warship of our college sports figures. Instead, we should put more emphasis on the students in the engineering and information systems departments.

Chinese people are putting more emphasis on their Information Technology studies in their colleges and universities and we are not. In my opinion, we devote too much time to college sports instead of developing our brainpower and Information Technology skills. Those skills would help us compete in today's economy with China. Chinese people have a book called **The Art of War.** This book was written by a Chinese philosopher Sun Tzu who follows that particular book to the letter. They realize that they will never defeat our militarily. But, eventually they will become more powerful than us. That is why we should focus less on our sports jocks and more on our geeks in the computer department, robotic departments, and even some medical departments as well. (Sue, n.d.)

For our college students to be successful in a university today, parents must have greater involvement in their children's education; especially in a college environment. For America to compete in the Global Economy today, America not only has to reform its education system. But it also has to stop or reduce the number of exchange students permitted in our universities. If not, let's face it those teachers and students from China that we have been discussing in this chapter will also steal our knowledge and technology. We as a nation will always be in second place in the world.

Some of you may call me a racist in this case. Nevertheless, I decided to include this particular issue in this specific chapter because even a simple Student Exchange Program has national security issues for the United States. Chinese people has a well-developed computer technology. They are hacking our computer systems and conducting industrial espionage. What does that mean? That means they are stealing, copying, and in some cases, reverse engineer our own technology which they can use against us.

Have you heard of an EMP weapon, for example?

What is an EMP weapon? EMP stands for an "Electrical Magnetic Pulse." This means Chinese people can computer hack our power grid. Then we would be years without power and nothing with electronics would function for years. (Conca, 2020)

Now, I will discuss the real problems that we face in today's education system from my perspective and some research on the subject. You have to realize that our education system was designed in the late 18th and early

19th Centuries. Our education system came to the United States with our German/Prussian immigrants. This particular education system was designed to teach you how to be obedient and how to be a good worker in a factory. That is correct, our education system was designed to produce good factory workers only. It was designed on the premises of memorization and remembering how to do certain tasks, because you needed it back then to remember the task you're going to perform in a factory.

The invention of the Internet and other electronic media that will help us in school. Then memorization and this education system of ours is basically obsolete. That is because we are relying more and more on computers and robotics. You see, nowadays even the best computer programmers look up things on the Internet. Of course, memorization is a good exercise to keep your mind active and it can help with many other things. But, when it comes to the job market, the memorization of useless information is unnecessary and it can be, as I said before, obsolete. What they should be teaching people in school today is how to look up information in books and onto the Internet and where you can find this particular information no matter what your subject may be or what you might have been studying. They should always teach you how to distinguish fake news versus real news. Also, they should teach you how to think and make your own judgments without pressure. In my opinion, people today cannot think on their own and make their own decisions because of our education system. They should always teach you how to manage your money and make decisions on savings for emergencies. Today's schools should teach you things that you will use in your everyday life and not teach you all the useless information we have today. I think; we should make our education reflect the needs of our society.

Your next question should be, can our education system be fixed? The answer to that particular question is yes. Your next question should be, who stands in the way of genuine reform of our educational system? There are many who stands in the way. Here I'm going to name a couple of them.

The first obstacle to Genuine Education Reform is your Teacher's Union. It's union bosses because the unions' union bosses have fancy houses, drive fancy cars, take vacations to the Bahama for example. They do this on the dues that the teachers pay to belong to the union.

The next obstacle to Genuine Education Reform is state loco in national politicians because the politicians regard our kids; they always have their hand in the cookie jar.

The last obstacle to the Genuine Education Reform in this country is the children's parents because they are not involved enough in their children's education, whether in primary school or through college.

I love it when there is a teacher's strike. When they get on the picket line, the teachers always say they have worked hard for little pay—what a bunch of crock that is. In my opinion, a teaching job in grade school, high school, and sometimes college is an easy job. That is because teachers usually work from September to June; they get summers off. If you have a lousy teacher that does not know how to teach, it is impossible to get them fired. That is because of our lovely Teacher's Union supports them. Look, kids, your teachers do not care about your success at the end of the day; all they care about is getting their paychecks every two weeks but teaching you anything useful that you will find helpful in your everyday living, forget about it. Nowadays, the school's job, in my opinion, is not to teach you but to make you think their way day do not want you in school to be a thinking individual for yourself. They want you to think their way. In my opinion, most people today go into teaching because it is an easy way to make a buck and this job of the teacher guarantees that the teacher will not get fired.

Next, some teachers may say, "I'm doing this job because I care about your children." When the teacher says that, you better think twice about that person and what they have said. Like I said before, all teachers care about is getting their paychecks every two weeks and about their union benefits. Nowadays, very few people go into the teaching profession because they genuinely want to help your child succeed.

CHAPTER 4

The Communists Are Coming

I know that I'm going to sound like Paul Revere when he was yelling, *"The British are coming!"* during our Revolutionary war in 1776. Now, I'm going to tell you something similar to what Paul Revere said, except this time I'm going to tell you that the Communists are coming. Since President Donald Trump did not win the election in 2020, America, in my opinion, will never be the same again.

I know that you are going to ask me a question, how can you say that the Communists are coming when we have elections every four years? May I say that you are asking a very interesting question. Therefore, I'm going to explain to you guys how this entire thing works. Let me give you an example so that you can see what I'm talking about. We all know that we had two previous presidents, George W. Bush was a Republican, and Barack Obama was a Democrat. This is where it gets really interesting, for this example. I'm going to use the Affordable Care Act, the law that was passed by a Democrat, Barack Obama, in which case yes, the next administration of Donald J. Trump has removed the mandate that you have to have insurance in this case, it is a very good thing. But, when we go in deeper into the Affordable Care Act and examine it a little bit closer, the so-called death panels are still there.

What does this mean for seniors and the older generation? That means that if you reach the old age of 70. For example, the doctor may tell you that treating your disease costs the insurance company too much money. In which case, it would be hard for you to get treatment for your illness in an ordinary hospital because of your age of 70. (2010). In my opinion, this particular Democratic Party is more dangerous to the American people that you will ever know. Here is why the Democratic/Leftist Party is dangerous to the United States. That is because they are not the Democrats of John F. Kennedy. Today's Democratic Party is funded and run by the Leftists and Communists.

Here are some examples of this.

1. The Democrats say that we will give everyone a free college education; sounds good, doesn't it? Aha, but here is the kicker in this game, we have to examine the quality of the college education that the Democrats are offering.

2. The middle class under the Democrats will pay a higher tax on their property and other things under the Democratic rule.

3. The most important thing is that the Democrats will give you this and that for free; but, they will create a dependent class of people on them.

See, none of you American people have lived under a Communistic System, but some of us have, especially the people in Eastern Europe.

The next question you should be asking yourself; who will pay for all this free stuff that the so-called Communist Democratic Party is going to give you? Well, in this case, you are the American voter and a taxpayer. The food will get so expensive that you will not be able to afford it. I know what you're going to say, but the food is expensive now in a store, yes, you are correct in this case, when we will have to somehow pay for all the things that the Communists and a Leftist would want to give everyone for free, the food in the grocery store will definitely cost more, and because of the taxes that the farmer/the American farmer will have to pay to the government, he will not be able to produce the necessary food to feed the whole entire nation.

This is where the real fun begins, that is because if the American farmer will not be able to produce the necessary food in order to feed the American population, because of the taxes that the American taxpayer will have to pay in order to keep giving things for free to the American people, this is where the shortages of food in the grocery store will begin and this is where our American ladies/wives will have to get up at 3:00 am to get ready to stand in line for everyday grocery items such as bread and some basic needs.

I know what you're thinking. Yes, that might be true, but that is not going to be a problem in the United States because we have such a thing as the food stamp program. Yes, you are correct to some degree, in this case. You have to understand that those welfare programs such as food stamps and other things were never designed to cope with everyone being on welfare.

Now we will discuss your own personal liberty that might be taken away from you by you, dear Democrats/Communists, because of the fairness doctrine. If they ever implemented your First Amendment on talk radio, for example, it will be gone. If you ever criticize the government on the Democrats, you will be labeled as a racist, a bigot, or a homophobe, and you'll be lucky if you don't end up in jail in this particular case.

Your Second Amendment will definitely be gone under the Democrats. We all know this is because one of the Democratic politicians has already said that he is coming for your guns. I know his name, but I cannot mention it because I cannot pronounce it correctly.

Believe me, since Joe Biden has been elected, this particular

Democratic politician will have a job in the Bidens administration.

I almost forgot, all the free stuff will not go to you as an American citizen, except it will go to that legal immigrant with a disease that will flood our country under the Democratic Joe Biden's administration. As an American citizen, you will be treated as a second-class citizen in your own country. I have a question for all you Leftist Communist Bombs.

If Joe Biden could not save our own GM manufacturing plant and or Chrysler plant here in Wilmington, Delaware, how you think he will save our own country and fix our American economy if he could not fix the problems in our own state economy in Delaware?

Do you notice something funny that in every state that's ran by the Democrats Leftist, nobody is opening a business? In that case, every business in a Democrat-ran state is shutting down and every job is leaving the state?

Some wise man told me that there is no free lunch in the real world. The faster you learn this, the better off you'll be.

CHAPTER 5

No Gold in Fort Knox

Since the 2008 financial crisis, I have been keeping an eye on commodities, like gold and other things. Lately, there has been speculation that there is no gold in the Fort Knox gold depository.

We have been hearing from people like Brian Meltzer on his show. Brian Meltzer decoded he interviewed some former employers that used to work in the Fort Knox gold depository, stating that there might not be gold in the gold depository. (2010) In this case, I do believe this gentleman, Brian Meltzer, that there is no gold in Fort Knox.

The United States national debt is $26 trillion, of course. This is not the actual number is an estimate. (htt3) https://www.usdebtclock.org/

Do you think this will ever get paid back? I don't think so. If for some reason, our gold has disappeared from the gold depository of Fort Knox, then our government has no choice but to print money out of thin air. Of course, there are several consequences to this endeavor; one of them is, if you print money out of thin air, then the money already in the system is worthless. This particular money will not buy you very much. The fall of the US dollar because of printing money our countries debt being around $26 trillion is a mathematical certainty. Some people say that there are no consequences to printing money. In this case, I do disagree with them.

Because of this financial emergency, many countries in Europe are asking for their money back in their gold deposits back from the Department of the US Treasury. This will lead us to inflation of prices in the grocery store. As you can see right now, the prices for basic items in the grocery store are very high. For example, today, $10 does not buy you many things in the grocery store. Back in the old days, when the dollar was worth something, $10 bought many more groceries. This will also lead to inflation and things like rent and property tax. As we all know, America has some problems with China, however, China does not have to fight us militarily. All they have to do is call on our financial obligation. In this case, America would have been in serious trouble. President Donald Trump tried to do his best to avoid this problem. Nonetheless, this will not lead to anything good.

You have to understand that because our global economy is so tightly linked with other countries' economies, if we fall, then economies around the world will suffer as well, some of us less, some of us more. It all depends on how those other countries prepared for this so-called economic collapse that is coming. It is only a question of time.

Your next question should be, what can an average citizen of the United States to prepare for this certain economic collapse?

1. Immediately put in some of your currency into gold.

2. Buy as much food and store it as possible.

3. Learn to live within your means and learn essential survival skills, if necessary.

There are several things that might lead to this so-called economic collapse. One of them might be the riots that we see in the streets right now; why do you say that?

As I mentioned in my other books, the left Communists/Democrats want to take this country and turn it upside down. You must understand some things: all your stock prices are being manipulated, gold prices as well. Remember this; nothing is what it seems.

Our ruling class does not care about ordinary United States citizens because they live in their own little bubble. Sometimes, they even create their own countries to separate themselves from an ordinary person or people. Because of their wealth, they can manipulate every part of our life. You have to understand their game planning, which is the name of the game, is control; because of their wealth, those particular people love to control through the media they owned and other things. The more the United States public gets informed on what's going on around them, we still have a chance to survive or even slow down even further the March of the global New World Order.

CHAPTER 6

The Chipping of Humanity

I have been doing this type of research, about globalism and the New World Order, for about 10 to 20 years. I have read a lot and watched a lot of YouTube videos on the subject of the New World Order and Global Governance, and this issue really tops the cake.

In Europe, in Sweden, people are willing to take FR ID chips under their skin. What's funny about this is how this is being sold to the European public as another one of those conveniences. What's even funnier is how people of Sweden are willing to have a chip put under their skin. When I read this article regarding this issue of chipping people on NPR, I thought this was just another propaganda piece NPR is known for. After careful research and verification of this particular story. In this case, the radio station NPR did an excellent job on this particular news item.

Some of you may say that the American people will never agree and will never take a chip under their skin no matter what conveniences this may offer. In this case, you are making a big mistake. That is because of the lack of knowledge by the American people and their dependents on technology. The American people will adopt and take a chip put under their skin for their so-called convenience. This particular technology should be strictly monitored in public should go and do their own research before they make their decision whether they want to be chipped or not.

I know what you can ask me right about now, are you against technology? Absolutely not, and here are the issues that concern is regarding the FRID chips that are being or will be placed under the human skin.

1. The privacy of information will be on those chips. Besides, this particular chip user will have access to this information because if someone else can access the information on your chip, you're just lost your private information.

2. There is the issue of basic income that the leftist Democrats are pushing, you see. If the American people take a chip under their skin, the problem is that the money might be deposited on those chips. In this case, the government and the globalist will have control over your life because, for example, say you will get a speeding ticket, turn off your chip, and not have access to your money example.

You can win the battles against the Globalists and the New World Order. In order to do that, the American people must stop being the sheep all that they are and take some responsibility for their actions. That is why in order for us to have any power against the globalists and the New World Order, you must have a very well educated and informed public.

There is another way that the American people are giving up their privacy for convenience in America and around the world.

Through the use of such things as Facebook, the American people realize that if the American people create a Facebook page, put their videos photos, and use the Facebook messenger to communicate with one another, they are losing the right to privacy.

Did you know that Mark Zuker Berg, the owner of Facebook, collects your personal data every time you use Facebook? His company shares the data with the NSA, and God knows who else.

I know what you're thinking, right about now, you telling us the Facebook users is that our personal information is compromised?

The answer to this particular question is an absolute yes because whatever app you use to communicate, whether on Facebook or any other platform, in reality, you have given up your right to privacy. You also must realize that, even if you delete your Facebook page, your photos and other things you have posted on your page are no longer yours. You have given your information to one of the globalists called Mark Zuckerberg. What surprises me in this game of convenience is that we are being sold. How do people around the world are willing to give up their own privacy? I think that the word privacy has lost its meeting in today's day and age.

In today's news, we hear that even the current President of the United States has no privacy when he talks to the leaders of other nations on behalf of the American people. Ladies and gentlemen, the day that we lose our privacy, this is the day that we have lost our nation, and there is no such thing as privacy in America anymore.

CHAPTER 7

Second Amendment Under Threat

In our Constitution of the United States, we as Americans have the Second Amendment that allows us, as free people, to keep and bear arms. After careful research and analysis, there is a significant threat to our Second Amendment rights.

When you go to purchase a firearm in a gun shop in America today, you must go through what we call a background check before you're allowed to purchase a firearm.

In this case, in my opinion, when you go, and you fill out the form to purchase a firearm, you are basically asking the government, the United States government, for permission basically to defend yourself and your property. If a person commits any type of crime with a firearm, you should be given the death penalty in that case, and I don't mean lethal injection in a prison setting. Executions for misuse of firearms, such as robbery, etc., should be carried out in public.

We have so much crime in this country because the American people have stopped being afraid of the punishment, and the parents have basically turned over the raising of their kids to the state. Suppose a United States citizen uses their firearm to defend themselves or himself and his family and property. In that case, this particular citizen should only have to call what we call a special pickup in that case. Our country, because of 50 years of liberal politics, has been turned upside down.

May I remind you that those liberals, who are basically soft on crime and tolerant of everything, are not liberals? They are what we call Judeo Communist Bolsheviks, and they do want to control everyone's life in the

United States.

If the American people do not wake up soon, we will lose all of our constitutional rights. You see that Communist Bolsheviks will not take away your rights all at once. They will do it quietly and in the dark.

Before I wrote this chapter, I was thinking about this issue for a very long time. As free people, we have the right to protect ourselves and our loved ones as well. As free people, we should not have to ask our dear government for permission if we decide to protect ourselves with firearms. In a free society, the government should be afraid of the people. Still, the people should not be afraid of the government, because let's face it, the government should work for the people but not people working for the government.

We, the American people, have to ask ourselves a question. Do we live in a free society anymore, or are we living under the New World Order already? The reason that we do have the Second Amendment to our Constitution, not only to go duck hunting, but we do have the Second Amendment to protect ourselves in case our government becomes a tyrant to the people and to our way of life.

Of course, this is not what you are being taught in your dear old public schools. That is because our so-called education system only wants you to be a good compliant sheep all and go quietly into the New World Order children should be taught gun safety in our public schools, and yes, if the teachers want to be armed in schools, then they should be allowed to do so. If we have an armed society, then we will have a free society.

The parents should be able to raise their kids as they see fit. The government should keep out of how the parents way and let the parents be parents except for child-abuse. In this case, we would have to redefine what child-abuse is. Because discipline, your child is not child-abuse at all. Because our parents were forced to abdicate their responsibilities as parents by our so-called left-leaning/do-gooder government, today's parents, because of this, have no control over their kids. Because of the fall of the nucleus of family values in today's society, the country of the United States will fall apart anyway. Is there a way to repair this system? The answer to that particular question is a definite yes; we can do this in a simpler way.

1. If the parents decide to have a child, there has to be parents and households.

2. One parent has to stay home and help raise that child, and the other parent must go to work to support the family. When one parent stays home, when a child comes home from school, that particular parent can sit down and help the child with their homework. When both parents work basically, your child is being raised by itself in the street.

I know that when one parent works and the other one stays home, there is less income for things. Before, the two parents decide to start a family. They actually have to decide the issue of can we do with less.

3. Parents have to be involved in the child's life throughout his entire academic life.

Basically, parents have to be parents, not your child's friend. The American people will have to become strong Americans, not this sheep all wishy-washy, society because if the American people don't do this, they will become slaves to the New World Order. That is what the New World Order wants.

CHAPTER 8

Who Stands Behind Our President?

Who do you think put President, Donald J. Trump in office? Yes, many people, including the president himself, like to say that he ran for the presidency by himself. That's okay, and that's cool. You must understand that nothing in Washington D.C. happens by chance or say so. Everything happens in Washington D.C. by design.

Okay then, who is behind the election of our president? I will answer the question for you. The people behind our president is a wealthy group of hedge fund managers called the Mercer's, who are the Mercer's you might be asking? The Mercer's are people who control some of the stock market things like Hedge funds of different companies and they do you sponsor some presidential candidate; in this case, they have sponsored the current Republican president. (2020) Like the Coke Brothers, the Mercer's are one of the two most billionaire families in America that basically control America and the world. Who are the Coke Brothers, you may ask? The Coke Brothers are just like the Mercer's and all the other wealthy families in America, that controls America and the world as well. The Mercer's and Coke Brothers have enough money to create their own countries if they so choose.

Why do you write about this? Might you be asking me right about now? That is because I want you to understand as a reader that everything happens for a reason and that most of the deals that affect most of our lives are decided behind closed doors that you don't even know about. (htt4)

I will be more than happy to provide you with additional information on who runs our elections as well as our political system in America today.

1. Blackstone Group is one of the groups that contribute money and resources to both parties. There are many others as well. In this case, what you must remember is that when certain groups of people contribute money to both political parties, especially in America today, those people have influences in our government. I understand that we were taught that we have a form of representative government in school, making us the United States of America, a republic. After you read this particular chapter, I bet you think differently. In my opinion, we cannot have a form of representative government when the richest and powerful can buy influences and favors from our government.

Remember this, ladies and gentlemen, if both parties agree on something, I mean the Republicans and the Democrats, we, the American people, at the end of the day, will be screwed. In my opinion, you cannot claim to be a representative government when the billionaires have all the say in a way the ordinary people will get nothing.

The representative form of government is basically fiction when the billionaires will tell you how things are going to be in reality. As an ordinary person, you don't have anything to say about it. (government secrets.org, n.d.) Because of the lack of civics classes in our schools today, the American people don't even understand how to research the candidates that they're going to vote for.

The American people also have to understand that elections do have consequences. Still, since the American people have been turned into the

American sheep all, I'm sure the New World Order will have no problem implementing their agenda. Right about now, you are asking yourself this question, can the New World Order agenda be stopped? The answer to that question is a definite yes; for this to be accomplished, the American education system must be reformed, and the people will have to be better informed about things that are going on around them.

There was one American President named John F. Kennedy, who tried to warn the American people in one of his speeches about the influence of the New World Order the speech was given in 1963 (Kennedy, 1963)

I wonder if the American people have taken President John F. Kennedy's warning seriously.

CHAPTER 9

Control of the Population by the Rich and Powerful

In this chapter in this book, I will discuss the population control that the rich and powerful are doing today to the entire human race. I thought when I started this research about the New World Order; I felt that when it came to population control by the rich and powerful, I thought it was a big joke. After careful research that took me years to understand, I know that the New World Order's population control is real; it is not a joke. It is relatively serious.

About 2 to 3 years ago, I heard about the Georgia guide stones and the state of Georgia, of course, but what was written on them gave me the shock of my life, especially the phrase "1. Maintain humanity under 500,000,000 in perpetual balance with nature." In my opinion, this is not only possible, but this is happening right in front of your eyes. Here is how this works, we all know that mega corporations produce the food and water that we drink in the food we eat. That are owned by the most influential people in the United States and around the world.

You also have to understand that half the American people are on some psychological or psychiatric drugs. In my previous book, I mentioned the American Holocaust on how this is being done through the pharmaceutical establishment.

Now is there a way to protect ourselves from the poison that our food is being raised on. Whether it's the meat products that we or anything that we put in our mouth? The answer to this particular question is an absolute yes. We can protect ourselves by growing our own food to the best of our ability. Of course, the people who live in the countryside are better prepared to do this because they may have enough room to raise chickens, grow and raise their own pigs, or even raise cows so that they can be self-sufficient in their needs for milk.

Now, what can we do to the ordinary folk who live in the city? For example, okay, in this case, you might not be able to do much. You can get a plot of land or adopt a plot of land that you already own. A good example of this could be your own backyard and you can grow your own vegetable garden and other fruits, so in this case, you can be self-sufficient in that particular sense. You can also learn herbal medicine through YouTube and other means such as books on that particular subject.

In order for you to survive in the city, things that are coming down the pike, the best way to do this is to become self-sufficient as much as possible. In this case, to become self-sufficient, the first thing is that you have to stop being lazy and have to put in the necessary work, for example, to grow a garden.

I would like to discuss with you this thing that the Communist Democrats are trying to push, which is the Socialized Medicine Concept. What is that mean? That means that your medical care would be basically free. Aha, here is the kicker to this game; most of the countries who have socialized medicine, for example, say you do need some sort of medical procedure. In that case, under their socialized medicine, you would have to wait months in order for you to get that procedure done under socialized medicine if you are an older person with a medical, condition then you just out of luck.

Here is an article that explains how socialized medicine and the New World Order work. (magazine, n.d.)

Of course, we all know that the rich and elite control all of the worlds and make decisions that affect us one way or the other. In America today, we have to tear, in my opinion, the medical system, one for the rich and powerful and one for the rest of them. This does not bother the rich and powerful because the rich have their own hospitals outside of the United States. One of the hospitals that do cater to the rich is located in Tijuana Mexico, yes, I know that you're about to laugh at me right about now. I will be more than happy to give you a particular link to that specific hospital. So, in that case, you can make your own judgment.

Let's get something straight here; I am not. I am not giving you medical advice. I am just showing you that the rich and powerful have their own medical system different from us because they have the money to do it.

In this case, I think it is time for the American people to stand up and be aware of things that are going on around them. (htt6)

The rich people have a different mindset then we do, because to the rich, we are just sheep all that's all, I know that this sounds harsh, but this is the God honest truth. One of the rich has bought out a cruise ship so that he and his cronies do not have to pay our US taxes, or they don't even have to associate with people like us. (htt7)

The only reason that the rich and the elite treat us like sheep is that we let them get away with it, and the reason is that the American people are just not informed or don't have access to the information.

I think if the American people want to be good productive citizens, it is essential for them to be informed about things that are going on around them to the best of their ability.

Look, ladies and gentlemen, there's nothing wrong with being wealthy. When the rich accumulate too much power, this is where we get into some trouble.

I forgot who, whoever said, that absolute power corrupts absolutely. Whoever said this was a very wise man. The rich are so powerful that in the old days, or even nowadays, rich people can even decide whether people with disabilities will live within our society or be locked away in some institution.

A local reporter named Bill Baldin reported on how people with disabilities were treated in 1968 in Pennsylvania. My question is that just because somebody is wealthy does not mean that he can play God.

Look, ladies and gentlemen, I am all for making money, and I do support capitalism. I even support what we call pure capitalism/non-restrictive capitalism. I understand there is a limit to what a rich person can do. Just because he has money, he is not always right. (htt12)

My question to you is we all know that these things were going on in 1968. How do we know that this stuff is not going on right now in 2020? So, I think that it is up to us to keep the richest and powerful people in check.

CHAPTER 10

Mind Control Experiments on the American People

The United States government, from the late 50s to the early 60s and even beyond, was doing mind-control experiments on the American citizens in the MK ultra-Central Intelligence Agency Program. That was designed to get someone to obey orders without any question or any type of feelings. (htt13) In this particular project, there were involved two men, Dr. Sidney Gottlieb, and the other gentleman's name was Frank Olson. There was also a medical officer from the United States Army in Fort Dietrich, Maryland. (htt14) (htt15) Does gentlemen war involved in my control experiments? Frank Olson lost his life in the service of our country under mysterious circumstances. There was one more person involved in the mind control experiment named Whitey Bulger. (htt16) Although he was a gangster and a hoodlum, Bolger, I don't think he knew the purpose of those experiments.

The MK ultra-experiments were shut down in 1973. As American citizens, we have to ask ourselves a question; they say that the MK ultra-program was shut down in 1973; why? Also, it makes me wonder if those types of programs are still going on under a different name and in other facilities? What's even more disturbing is that the poor American people are not aware of these things. Of course, the American people are not entitled to know everything that is going on within our government. When it comes to ordinary American citizens' lives, this is where we should draw the line.

Even President John F. Kennedy said in his speech in 1961 when he said, "That secrecy is repugnant." (htt17)

I understand that some American people are just not interested and what our government does. Nevertheless, it is our responsibility as American citizens to keep our government in check, especially regarding our citizens' well-being. Therefore, in this case, what I want to do is pull the curtain a little bit so that the American people will get interested in what is going on around them.

The elite ruling class can only implement the New World Order plans if the American people look the other way. Supposed we as American citizens can take a little bit of responsibility and be more informed. In that case, the New World Order will have a tough time implementing its notorious agenda for humanity.

I think the American people are entitled to be free and well informed. One wise man said for the evil to succeed is when good people do nothing. Due to my knowledge about this particular issue, sometimes it makes me wonder if some of those school shootings that recently happened under the Barack Obama administration were not caused by the people under the mind control from somewhere else. Look, I know that this might be the only speculation on my part because I still live in a free country, but I can still analyze and have my own opinion on issues.

Most of those projects and the budget for those projects are under the Pentagon of the US government. (htt18) They will not disclose those types of money that are going to those projects; this type of cash would be labeled under the miscellaneous things. It is different when you volunteer for these types of projects, such as MK ultra-when you are being experimented on like a guinea pig by your government as a US citizen, then this changes the entire ballgame.

Some international citizens, such as the French, were unaware that they were being used as guinea pigs in the MK ultra-experiments (htt19). Therefore, US citizens and citizens around the world should be aware of some things that their government is doing in their name.

CHAPTER 11

The First Earth Battalion

Col. Jim Channon started the First Earth Battalion. He was part of the United States Special Forces in the early 60s through the late 70s and even to the early 80s.

He taught his men how to defend themselves with lethal weapons and how to use their minds to defend themselves. (htt20) As it turns out, this concept of the First Earth Battalion Program is still being taught to the U.S. Army Special Forces.

So, what you're saying is, do the Jedi Knights still exist?

They are not really Jedi Knights; they understand almost the same concepts. There is speculation out there that general James Matus went through the First Earth Battalion training under Lt. Col. Jim Channon's tutelage. Yes, the same general James Matus who served as an advisor to President Donald J. Trump. That concept of a warrior monk is not a foreign concept because the first people to practice their way were your Shaolin monks, who perfected a warrior monk's idea. (htt24)

So, who was Lt. Col., Jim Channon?

Jim Channon was born September 10, 1939; he served in the U.S. Army Special Forces from 1962 through 1982 officially. He did some consulting for the U.S. Army, as well as for companies like AT&T and DuPont, among other things. (htt25) So what you're saying is that those men who went through the First Earth Battalion Program training can move objects with their mind; all I'm saying is that that might be a possibility.

We all remember the United States Army's slogan, back in the early

90s, *"Be All You Can Be"* Lt. Col. Jim Channon came up with this slogan.

The First Earth Battalion Program has not shut down. These concepts of nonlethal use of force are still being taught to the United States Special Forces teams today. You have to understand that yes, in some cases, the government does shut down some programs. A program like the First Earth Battalion has not shut down, but it has been moved to a different facility and is still taught to the U.S. Army personnel who go through Special Forces Training in some cases.

You have to understand that those programs do exist. Our government should be a little bit more transparent in this case. For example, they should tell us that yes, this program or that program does exist. They should leave it at that, that is because I think we can all understand that we cannot allow people or enemies from around the world to know what we have or we don't have as capability. This way, when they say yes, we do have a program like the First Earth Battalion, for example. They should not give us any more information but that. That is because that is the best way to deal with that particular issue.

CHAPTER 12

9/11 was an Inside Job

I know that this might be one of the most controversial chapters in my book. This does require some discussion and a little better thinking. To understand this chapter, you will have to turn off your emotions and put on your analytical and thinking abilities. Several issues have to be addressed when we are discussing the terrorist attacks from September 11, 2001.

The number one question should be, was 9/11 an inside job?

After careful analysis and doing some extensive research on this particular subject, I have reluctantly concluded that, yes, 9/11 had to be an inside job. Here are my reasons why I came to this conclusion.

1. Where was our border and immigration services? The question is, why did those people who supposedly carried out the 9/11 attacks able to get into our country in the first place?

2. How come our fighting jets were not scrambled? Also, why weren't those planes that hit the World Trade Center and the Pentagon shot down? The procedure for responding to this type of incident is a war in place since the Eisenhower administration where a pilot can shoot down an airplane if he does not respond to his verbal or light communications. Therefore, how come this procedure was not appropriately executed on that particular day?

3. On September 10, Donald Rumsfeld, the secretary of defense under the Bush Administration, said that 2.3 trillion dollars were missing from the Pentagon. When they said on the news that a second plane hit the Pentagon, this was not a plane because they have not found a fuselage or a

wheel or any part of the airplane that hit the Pentagon. In this chapter, I'm going to include a piece of speech that Donald Rumsfeld said to CBS News on September 10, 2001. (News 2012) This is why we, the American people, must keep our elected officials in check.

Who do you think is responsible for the 9/11 attack? The answer might be the people who are responsible for 9/11. It could be our own government, that is because, after careful research, I can only make one conclusion. Throughout this whole deal, our government has caused 9/11 to pass things like Homeland Security and the Patriot Act. It may be clear these acts do not have anything to do with your Homeland Security. All they do is infringe on our freedoms and liberties.

Maybe those planes that hit the Twin Towers were piloted by remote control; this is possible. All we have to do is look at Operation Aphrodite during World War II, where or B-17s were piloted by remote control.

I know that some of my critics' of mine I agree with my conclusions. We have to remember that they did not have the best equipment to do this kind of work back then. We will have to remember that this type of equipment that was placed in those bombers nowadays can be miniaturized. This type of operation could have been carried out that way. (htt26)

Of course, when it comes to 9/11, we will not know the real truth. There are people in the higher-ups who noted the truth, but they will not tell us. This is because the American people know nothing but sheep all to the Ruling Class. I notice with the Ruling Class that the politicians who claim to represent us, whether on the local level or in Washington D.C., separate themselves from us that people will put them in office.

So, in this case, we don't know what is going on behind the curtain. Of course, once in a while, we can get a peek or sneak peek for that matter to see what is going on, but only for a moment. I understand that some good people will tell us what is going on behind the curtain once in a while. One of those people who has been doing a good job, in my opinion, is Alex Jones. Such people like Alex Jones, Dr. Michael Savage is being laughed at when they present their evidence. So, in this case, I am saying after my careful research on this particular subject, I would say that yes the 9/11 was an inside job because the Ruling Class wanted to enslave us by the Patriot Act. They also brought down the economy of the United States. Ask yourself this particular question, has the Academy since the 9/11 attacks improved or declined, whether we had a Republican President or a Democrat? The American people will not start this particular Civil War. The Leftist Communists' Bombs will start this Civil War, **people who think they are entitled to everything and everything should be given to them for free. When you start taking things from the rich, the rich can leave the country altogether. Then what are the American people left with; absolutely nothing.**

Let me make one thing clear I do not, let me repeat, I do not want a civil war in this country. This is not up to us; this will depend on how the Leftist Communists will react to our next presidential election. All I want to do in my books is to show you that nothing is what it seems. Nothing in Washington D.C. and around the world happens by chance; it all happens by design. Yes, some people do control everything that happens in this world. There are about 12 wealthiest families that do have the power to do that.

CHAPTER 13

The Fall of the Republic

The power of those people who control the world is tremendous. Those people who control the world have the power to get rid of a sitting United States President if they do not follow their agenda. Yes, they tried to get rid of President Donald J. Trump, but the way they when about it was interesting in itself. They would have accomplished this by hacking our electronic voting machines. President Donald Trump believes that is why he lost the election to Joe Biden due to the hacking of the electronic voting machines.

Your question should be, are you sure about that?

The answer to this particular question is an absolute yes. I am very sure of this. It does not cost very much actually to hack the voting machines of today. That is because our voting machines are nothing more than computers with their own operating systems. We also know that the Leftist Democratic/Communist Party has an unlimited supply of money. So yes, they did hack our computer voting machines. I will even give you reference material so that you can make your own judgment about this.

This is for your order Americans and people with disabilities. Once the Democrat/Communist Party gets into power, they will Institute specific laws that the older people and people with disabilities will have a tough time getting the medical treatment when the socialized medicine goes into effect thanks to the Democrat Bolshevik Party. I do not blame the people with disabilities for this when it comes to the older generation; they are the ones who are responsible for the state of affairs as they are at this point.

So how do you think our election was stolen? (Semantic 20)

When in this chapter, I have said that the United States as a Republic is dead, that is not a joke. That is the genuine, honest truth. When God threatens our most fundamental right in America, the right to vote knows who, then, unfortunately, our country as a republic is finished. We are in big trouble than any other so-called Banana Republic because we seize to exist once we vote. Then we as the American people eventually cease to exist as a nation as well. That is because the levels of corruption have to be accepted. When the corruption reaches a certain level, the country slips into anarchy and ceases to be a nation.

I know what you are thinking; you're saying that we have a Constitution here in the United States. You are right; however, when you can manipulate a national election, the Bolsheviks/Communists will exploit this advantage and use the power of the vote to get their agenda. Sooner or later, believe it or not, because of this, they will try to change our Constitution and not for the better but for the worse.

Whether you are the middle class, in America or upper-middle-class, or even the poor, you will suffer equally under the regime of Communist/Bolsheviks because the rich people do have the money and the resources to start their own lives over in another country. The middle class and the poor will suffer in that case that is because, in a Communist/Bolshevik nation, those people on top of the system will have everything; the people in the middle and the lower economic scale will suffer the most. Wealthy people can manipulate the system to make it better for themselves but not for the rest of the population. Things like unemployment and poverty will be the norm; it will not be the exception.

As I said before, those welfare programs are not designed to be long-term stable, when many people are forced to use the welfare system because of the lack of jobs. That will happen under the Bolshevik government, and then the welfare system will collapse.

Of course, the Democrat/Bolsheviks Party does have the money to do this, so in this case, yes, absolutely, they could have paid for the manipulation of our votes through the computer and electronic voting machines. So, in this case, we did lose our Constitutional Republic because if you can control the ballot box and the vote, you can control America. Therefore, the genuine losers, in this case, will be the American people. You have to understand that the most vulnerable in the middle class will suffer the most under the rule of the Democrat Bolsheviks.

In America, there is no free lunch; even year free college education will not be free because someone eventually will have to pay for it, and in that case, the quality of the free college education, in this case, will suffer.

I know what you are thinking, if the situation in America gets real bad, then the rich will suffer just like the rest of us.

You are very wrong in this case because the rich have enough money to live anywhere they want to.

They have their own private schools for their kids; they have their own hospitals outside of the United States where they can go for treatment when necessary. You see, they live in their own little bubble separate from the rest of us. Like I said before, the name of their game is control, which means they do like to control the world, and most of the laws that they pass it is to benefit them. This does not benefit all of us, the ordinary American citizens.

The information that I can provide in this particular book can help you so that you can not only thrive and survive in the New World Order, but you will be able to prosper as well because you will know what to do by reading my book.

On the other hand, if we all act like that's all get the rich, then, in that case, we will all lose, that is because whatever you may say about the rich, the rich will always create their jobs that we need to survive so yes in this case the rich do control our nation. None the less, we do need them to be able to live and survive this time. Yes, for sure, those wealthy people are rich, some of them or even superrich. As human beings, you do not have to let them walk all over you.

Your next question will be, was Donald Trump part of the New World Order?

In this case, I will say that he had to work within the system. He saw the danger of the New World Order, that is why the globalists and the Communists are trying to get rid of President Donald J. Trump as of this writing. If our elections in America will be proven legitimate or corrupted, then we are worse than any of the South American Banana Republics.

There is nothing with trying or baying rich. When the rich get too much power, that is when the situation can, and it does get out of control.

In my opinion, knowledge is power, and by reading my books. I hope that the knowledge that I have provided for you will help you adapt to the upcoming situation because I will guarantee you will be able to survive and drive and maybe even make a positive impact on your situation.

If you are going to be educated on the word New World Order and have the knowledge necessary, you will survive what is coming in this country.

Nothing in America after this presidential election will be the same. There is no reason for you to panic about the situation because when you read this book, you will be able to know what to do when the situation arises.

This situation that is coming in the United States is nothing to fear except you have to be prepared for the upcoming tribulations.

You have to understand that what will happen to us; it does not bother the Communist Bolsheviks. That is because those Bolsheviks and Communists will have their own stores, where they will have everything from the Coca-Cola products to whatever their heart desires. You're the ordinary person who will end up with nothing.

Those people who will be part of the comer's Bolshevik Apparatus will live in luxury. You, as an ordinary US citizen, will have to do with less.

If you have a job, of course, you're going to make $15 an hour, you think that's cool okay, but here is the kicker to this game, if you are making $15 an hour, and your food in the grocery store cost you twice or three times as much, then you will be set back financially twice or three times as much.

Your electric bill will go up significantly in price. What you will have to worry about is when the new environmental policies and other policies will be implemented, your lifestyles will change dramatically, the Bolshevik Communists will be able to do anything they want, but you will be eventually paying the pipe for that.

What seems to amaze me personally is how gullible the American people are when the Democrat/Communist Party promises the American people everything for free and how fast they are willing to give up their own liberties and rights as US citizens.

Remember this the Democrats might give you this or that for free. Eventually, you're going to pay for it one way or the other.

Some of us who have lived in the communist/Bolshevik system we know what's it all about. When it comes to the American people, they will not learn anything until they experience the Bolshevik Communist System on their own.

If this weren't so serious, it would have been funny how the American people do not understand how the Communist Bolshevik System works. Those people at the top of the food chain will have everything because they will have their own stores where to buy things, but the ordinary people will be lucky to get scraps of potato peels to eat.

The Democrat Bolsheviks will not change the Constitution legally at all. They will use their own local laws to do this because the American people will be getting their stuff for free. When you start losing First Amendment rights, the American people will not say anything. Therefore, in that case, this is what the Democrats want to do with us. They want to turn us into the obedient sheep all so that they can implement their global communist New World Order, in which your personal freedoms will be curtailed even eliminated. Even if people try to speak out, those people will be silent. This is already happening for those of you who are using platforms on Social Media such as Facebook and YouTube. This is how the Bolsheviks/Communists will take away your right of freedom of speech. Unfortunately, the American people will gladly give up their personal liberties. The name of free stuff, colleges, and universities will not be a place where you can exchange your ideas. Those universities and colleges will become brainwashed institutions where you'll be taught how to think their way.

The biggest winner of this will be an illegal immigrant but not a United States citizen. That is because the big technology companies such as Google and Apple found a way to hire more illegal immigrants in the computer and technology field than American. (Dice 2020)

as we are sitting here, the Bolsheviks Democrats are already working on ways to reverse the employment policy, so it's more beneficial to the tech workers from other countries than our own US citizens.

This is happening because the Democrat Bolsheviks know very well that the American people are not well informed about the situation. Therefore, they're already making plans to implement their policies.

I know what you're thinking, you may say to yourself, my family is poor anyway, so in this case, what do I care if the government gives me things for free.

Well, understand this, if you are poor, now think about how poor you are going to be when you have one salami to buy in the butcher shop, or your food stamps will not be enough to buy much of anything because of food price inflation. What is the definition of food price inflation? The actual meaning of food price inflation is (2020). Food inflation refers to the condition whereby an increase in the wholesale price index of an essential food item is defined as a food basket relative to the general inflation or the consumer price index. Therefore, no matter what job you will have, your pay will not keep up with the price increase, especially when it comes to price inflation, especially for food and other essential items.

So, what should we do as American citizens?

You would have to start saving money, do not put all of your savings in one basket. Buy and store essential food items, learn skills like carpentry and other trades to use them, to earn a living post-collapse of the economy.

You have to prepare yourself spiritually and mentally for what is coming because there will be some difficult times during the upcoming years.

Of course, those times will not be this easy. What some minimal preparation, you will have a chance to survive and positively impact your community.

ABOUT THE AUTHOR

Mark Wrobel

Mark Wrobel resides in Wilmington, Delaware, and he was born with a disability. But it didn't allow that to stop him from excelling in life.

His father raised Mark; he was a dedicated single parent. He grew up in a communist system. Due to his disability, his country would not allow him to attend school with regular kids, but he persevered.

Fortunately, when he was about 10-years-old, he came to the United States, which he knew was the land of opportunity. So, he took full advantage of it and made sure he got a good education.

From 1989 until 1993, he attended St. Thomas The Apostle School, a Catholic school in Wilmington, Delaware.

Then in 1993, he attended Wilmington High School and graduated in 1997 with a high school diploma.

In 2002, Mark attended Delaware Tech Community College to attend their Web Designer Certificate Program, which he completed.

He continued his education in 2008 at Strayer University, studying Information Systems and Homeland Security. Mark graduated from Stayer in 2012 with an Associate Degree.

In 2018, he returned to Strayer University to obtain his Bachelor of Science Degree in Information Systems and Homeland Security Management and graduated in 2020. He is proud of this accomplishment because he was told that it was impossible and he couldn't do it.

Mark is currently employed with the United States Coast Guards in Communications. He began working for the Coast Guard in 2012. Thus far, he has received multiple awards and accolades for his dedicated service. Mark loves to learn and try new things.

In 2007, he decided to try sky diving, and with the help of an instructor, he jumped 18,000 feet. There was an article published about it in the News Journal.

In the future, he would like to go back to school to obtain his master's and a doctoral degree.

Mark is the author of the title Progressive Credentialism Versus Ageism and The American Holocaust, which are available online worldwide. This is his third book, and he couldn't have done it without his father's support.

REFERENCES

People who are responsible for the upcoming Civil War:
- Timothy Leary https://en.wikipedia.org/wiki/Timothy_Leary
- William Kunstler https://en.wikipedia.org/wiki/William_Kunstler
- George Soros https://en.wikipedia.org/wiki/George_Soros

Georgia guide stones and control the population:
- https://en.wikipedia.org/wiki/Georgia_Guidestones
- https://thetvtraveler.com/visiting-the-georgia-guidestones/

The power of money which the rich controls the population:
- https://www.bing.com/videos/search?q=the+population+control+the+history+channel&docid=607989188491936229&mid=0E58E9D3F304AD2364790E58E9D3F304AD236479&view=detail&FORM=VIRE

You have the rich control you because of the money that they have:
- https://www.bing.com/videos/search?q=The+power+of+money+Americas+book+of+secrets+the+history+channel&docid=608030042266208501&mid=B4BF2F6C4CACFFB41FABB4BF2F6C4CACFFB41FAB&view=detail&FORM=VIRE
- https://heavy.com/entertainment/2019/10/pennhurst-asylum/
- https://www.history.com/shows/americas-book-of-secrets-special-edition/season-1/episode-4

Here is where the rich go if they need medical care:

- http://www.cancure.org/11-list-of-clinics-in-the-united-states-offering-alternative-therapies/clinics-outside-of-the-us/107-international-bio-care-hospital-and-medical-center-ibc

The chipping the of humanity:

- https://www.npr.org/2018/10/22/658808705/thousands-of-swedes-are-inserting-

Microchips-under-their-skin:

- https://www.youtube.com/watch?v=qWVQR99bXt8

Here is how the American tech workers will lose their jobs:

- https://insights.dice.com/2020/11/12/tech-immigration-h-1b-reform-on-the-way-most-big-tech-employees-think/?amp&utm_campaign= Advisory_ DiceAdvisor _H1B&utm_source=Responsys&utm_medium=Email

Operation MK ultra-mind control:

- https://www.history.com/topics/us-government/history-of-mk-ultra
- https://www.thedailybeast.com/did-the-cias-dr-frank-olson-jump-to-his-death-or-was-he-pushed
- https://en.wikipedia.org/wiki/Sidney_Gottlieb
- https://en.wikipedia.org/wiki/Project_MKUltra
- https://en.wikipedia.org/wiki/Frank_Olson
- https://allthatsinteresting.com/james-whitey-bulger-mk-ultra

- https://www.theatlantic.com/technology/archive/2010/03/did-the-cia-really-dose-a-french-village-with-lsd/346370/

No gold in Fort Knox:

- https://www.imdb.com/title/tt2066343/
- https://www.usdebtclock.org/
- https://en.wikipedia.org/wiki/Gold_repatriation

First Earth Battalion:

- https://en.wikipedia.org/wiki/First_Earth_Battalion#:~:text=The%20First%20Earth%20Battalion%20was%20the%20name%20proposed,supersoldiers%20to%20be%20organized%20along%20New%20Age%20lines.
- https://en.wikipedia.org/wiki/Jim_Channon
- https://en.wikipedia.org/wiki/Jim_Mattis
- https://en.wikipedia.org/wiki/Shaolin_Monastery

American Democracy no longer exists:

- https://www.youtube.com/watch?v=wmoxE1sJc1c

Here are the biggest families who control America and the world:

- https://en.wikipedia.org/wiki/Koch_family
- https://nymag.com/intelligencer/2019/06/the-mercer-family-has-reportedly-bailed-on-trump-in-2020.html
- https://en.wikipedia.org/wiki/Robert_Mercer
- https://www.opensecrets.org/elections-overview/top-organizations

Socialized medicine in America:

- https://www.forbes.com/sites/johngoodman/2019/03/05/what-socialized-medicine-looks-like/?sh=7a1abe7f625b
- https://www.kff.org/health-reform/fact-sheet/summary-of-the-affordable-care-act/

Positive role models for the Black community:

- https://en.wikipedia.org/wiki/Mary_Jackson_(engineer)
- https://en.wikipedia.org/wiki/Tuskegee_Airmen
- https://en.wikipedia.org/wiki/Frederick_Douglass

So-called Black leadership:

- https://en.wikipedia.org/wiki/Al_Sharpton
- https://en.wikipedia.org/wiki/Jesse_Jackson

Church burning in Washington, D.C.:

- https://www.pacificpundit.com/2020/05/31/st-johns-church-in-washington-d-c-set-on-fire-by-leftists-antifa/
- https://delawarebusinessnow.com/2020/05/floyd-protest-spreads-to-i-95-in-wilmington/
- https://www.thechesapeaketoday.com/2020/06/03/looting-in-delaware-gang-caught-in-the-act-of-looting-walmart/

EMP weapon:

- https://heavy.com/news/2020/06/peter-pry-china-emp-attack/

9/11 was an inside job:

- https://www.youtube.com/watch?v=IVpSBUgbxBU
- https://en.wikipedia.org/wiki/Operation_Aphrodite

www.ingramcontent.com/pod-product-compliance
Lightning Source LLC
Chambersburg PA
CBHW062200100526
44589CB00014B/1891